Arduino

The Complete Beginner's Guide

Byron Francis

© 2016

Table Of Contents

Introduction

I want to thank you and congratulate you for downloading the book, *"Arduino: The Complete Beginner's Guide"*.

This book contains proven steps and strategies on how to you started on the road to creating things using micro-controllers. We will discuss only enough electronics for you to make the circuits, and only enough programming for you to get started. The focus will be on your making things. It is my hope that as you go through this book you will be flooded with ideas of things that you can make. So let's get going...Thanks again for downloading this book, I hope you enjoy it!

Chapter 1

Getting Started

The purpose of this book is to get you started on the road to creating things using micro-controllers. We will discuss only enough electronics for you to make the circuits, and only enough programming for you to get started. The focus will be on your making things. It is my hope that as you go through this book you will be flooded with ideas of things that you can make. So let's get going... The first question we'll start with is:

1.1 What is a Microcontroller?

Wikipedia1 says:

A micro-controller is a small computer on a single integrated circuit containing a processor core, memory, and programmable input/output peripherals

The important part for us is that a micro-controller contains the processor(which all computers have) and memory, and some input/output pins that you can control. (often called GPIO - General Purpose Input Output Pins).

For this book, we will be using the Arduino Uno board. This combines a micro-controller along with all of the extras to make it easy for you to build and debug your projects.

We will be using a breadboard in this book. This is a relatively easy way to make circuits quickly. Breadboards are made for doing quick experiments. They are not known for keeping circuits together for a long time. When you are ready to make a project that you want to stay around for a while, you should consider an alternative method such as wire-wrapping or soldering or even making a printed circuit board (PCB). The first thing you should notice about the breadboard is all of the holes. These are broken up into 2 sets of columns and a set of rows

1.2 Install the Software

the rows are divided in the middle. The columns are named a, b, c, d, e, f, g, h, i, and j (from left to right). The rows are numbered 1 - 30. (from top to bottom). The columns on the edges do not have letters or numbers. The columns on the edges are connected from top to bottom inside of the breadboard to make it easy to supply power and ground. (You can think of ground as the negative side of a battery and the power as the positive side.) For this book our power will be +5 volts. Inside of the breadboard, the holes in each row are connected up to the break in the middle of the board. For Example: a1,b1,c1,d1,e1 all have a wire inside of the breadboard to connect them. Then f1, g1, h1, i1, and j1 are all connected. but a1 is not connected to f1. This may sound confusing now, but it will quickly come to make sense as we wire up circuits.

1.2 Install the Software

If you have access to the internet, there are step-by-step directions and the software available at: http://arduino.cc/en/Main/Software Otherwise, the USB stick in your kit2 has the software under the Software Directory. There are two directories under that. One is "Windows" and the other is "Mac OS X". If you are installing onto Linux, you will need to follow the directions at: http://arduino.cc/en/Main/Software

1.2.1 Windows Installations

1. Plug in your board via USB and wait for Windows to begin its driver installation process. After a few moments, the process will fail. (This is not unexpected.)

2. Click on the Start Menu, and open up the Control Panel.

3. While in the Control Panel, navigate to System and Security. Next, click on System. Once the System window is up, open the Device Manager.

4. Look under Ports (COM & LPT). You should see an open port named "Arduino UNO (COMxx)".

5. Right click on the "Arduino UNO (COMxx)" port and choose the "Update Driver Software" option.

6. Next, choose the "Browse my computer for Driver software" option.

7. Finally, navigate to and select the Uno's driver file, named "ArduinoUNO.inf", located in the "Drivers" folder of the ArduinoSoftware download (not the "FTDI USB Drivers" sub-directory).

8. Windows will finish up the driver installation from there.

9. Double-click the Arduino application.

10. Open the LED blink example sketch: File > Examples > 1.Basics > Blink

11. Select Arduino Uno under the Tools > Board menu.

12. Select your serial port(if you don't know which one, disconnect the UNO and the entry that disappears is the right one.)

13. Click the Upload button.

14. After the message "Done uploading" appears, you should see the "L" LED blinking once a second. (The "L" LED is on the Arduino directly behind the USB port.)

1.2.2 Mac Installation

1. Connect the board via USB.

2. Drag the Arduino application onto your hard drive.

3. When Network Preferences comes up, just click "Apply" (remember the /dev/tty/usb.)

4. Start the program.

1.3 The Integrated Development Environment (IDE)

5. Open the LED blink example sketch: File > Examples > 1.Basics > Blink

6. Select Arduino Uno under the Tools > Board menu.

7. Select your serial port(if you don't know which one, disconnect the UNO and the entry that disappears is the right one.)

8. Click the Upload button.

9. After the message "Done uploading" appears, you should see the "L" LED blinking once a second. (The "L" LED is on the Arduino directly behind the USB connection)

1.3 The Integrated Development Environment (IDE)

You use the Arduino IDE on your computer (picture following) to create, open, and change sketches (Arduino calls programs "sketches". We will use the two words interchangeably in this book.). Sketches define what the board will do. You can either use the buttons along the top of the IDE or the menu items.

Parts of the IDE: (from left to right, top to bottom)

• Compile - Before your program "code" can be sent to the board, it needs tobe convertedintoinstructions thatthe board understands. This process is called compiling.

• Stop - This stops the compilation process. (I have never used this button and you probably won't have a need to either.)

• Create new Sketch - This opens a new window to create a new sketch.

• Open Existing Sketch - This loads a sketch from a file on your computer.

1.4 Our first circuit

• Save Sketch - This saves the changes to the sketch you are working on.

• Upload to Board - This compiles and then transmits over the USB cable to your board.

• Serial Monitor - We will discuss this in section 5.1.

• Tab Button - This lets you create multiple files in your sketch. This is for more advanced programming than we will do in this class.

• Sketch Editor - This is where you write or edit sketches

• Text Console - This shows you what the IDE is currently doingand is also where error messages display if you make a mistake in typing your program. (often called a syntax error)

• Line Number - This shows you what line number your cursor is on. It is useful since the compiler gives error messages with a line number

1.4 Our first circuit

Before we get to the programming, let's connect an LED. LED stands for Light Emitting Diode. A diode only allows electricity to flow through it one way, so if you hook it up backwards it won't work. If you connect the LED directly to power and ground, too much current will go through the diode and destroy it. To keep that from happening we will use a resistor to limit the current. You can think of a resistor like a water pipe. The higher the value of the resistor is like using a smaller pipe that lets less electric- ity "flow" through. This is not technically correct, but it is close enough for this book. We will use a 330 Ohm (Ohm is often shown as Ω) resistor (Resistance is measured in ohms. Resistors have color bands on them that let you know what value they are.3 A 330Ω resistor will have color bands: Orange-Orange-Brown) It doesn't matter which way you plug in a resistor. The two leads (sometimes called "legs") of an LED are called an anode and a cathode. The anode is the longer lead. IMPORTANT: IF YOU PLUG IT IN

3We are not going to talk in this text about how to decide which size resistor to use.

Chapter 1 Getting Started

BACKWARDS, IT WILL NOT WORK. (But it won't be damaged, either. Don't worry.)

1. With a wire, connect ground from the Arduino (labeled GND) to the bottom row of the farthest right column of the bread board.

2. With a wire, connect power from where it says 5V (the V stands for volt- age and this is where the electric power comes from.) on the Arduino to the bottom row of the next to right column.

3. Connect the resistor with one end in h2 and the other end on the far right column (ground).

4. Connect the LED cathode (shorter leg) to f2. (This makes it connect to the resistor through the breadboard because they are on the same row.)

5. Connect the LED anode (longer leg) to f3.

6. Connect a wire from h3 to the next to right column (+5V).

7. Plug power into the Arduino.

8. The LED should light up. If it doesn't, unplug power from the Arduino, check all of your connections and make sure you have not plugged the LED in backwards. Then try power again.

Congratulations, you have made your first circuit!

1.5 Updated Circuit

Let's modify our circuit slightly so that the Arduino will be controlling the LED. Take the wire from h3 and connect it to pin 13 of the Arduino. You could use any pin, we are using pin 13 because the default program on the Arduino when you first get it blinks the "L" LED which is on pin 13 so we can check our circuit without any new software. (You should unplug your Arduino before making changes to the circuit.)

1.6 Our First Program

Now let's write a program to control the LED. Each program must contain at least two functions. A function is a series of programming statements that can be called by name.

1. setup() which is called once when the program starts.

2. loop() which is called repetitively over and over again as long as the Arduino has power.

So the shortest valid Arduino program (even though it does nothing) is:

Listing 1.1: Simplest Program

```
1 void setup()
2 { 3 }
4 5 void loop() 6 { 7 }
```

In most programming languages, you start with a program that simply prints "Hello, World" to the screen. The equivalent in the micro-controller world is getting a light to blink on and off. This is the simplest program we can write to show that everything is functioning correctly. (Throughout this book we will show the program (sketch) in its entirety first, and then explain it afterwards. So if you see something that doesn't make sense, keep reading and hopefully it will be cleared up.)

Listing 1.2: led1/led1.pde 1 const int kPinLed = 13;

```
2 3 void setup() 4 { 5 pinMode(kPinLed, OUTPUT); 6 }
```

```
7 8 void loop() 9 { 10 digitalWrite(kPinLed, HIGH); 11 delay(500); 12 digitalWrite(kPinLed, LOW); 13 delay(500); 14 }
```

Here is a breakdown of what this program does.

1 const int kPinLed = 13;

This defines a constant that can be used throughout the program instead of its value. I HIGHLY encourage this for all pins as it makes it easy to change your software if you change your circuit. By convention, constants are named starting with the letter k. You don't have to do this, but it makes it easier when you look through your code to know what is a constant.

3 void setup() 4 { 5 pinMode(kPinLed, OUTPUT); 6 }

This sets up the pin that our LED is connected to as an OUTPUT pin. (Meaning that the Arduino is controlling "writing" to a pin instead of reading from it.)

8 void loop() 9 { 10 digitalWrite(kPinLed, HIGH); 11 delay(500); 12 digitalWrite(kPinLed, LOW); 13 delay(500); 14 }

These lines are where the action is. We start by writing HIGH out on the pin connected to the LED which will turn the LED on. (HIGH means putting 5V out on the pin. The other choice is LOW which means putting 0V out on the pin.) We then call delay() which delays the number of milliseconds (1 1000th of a second) sent to it. Since we send the number 500, it will delay for½second. We then turn the LED off by writing LOW out on the pin. We delay for 500 milliseconds (½second) This will continue until power is removed from the Arduino. Before we go any further, try this on your Arduino and make sure it works. (there is an LED on the UNO board that is connected to pin 13 so if it blinks and your LED on the breadboard doesn't, then you probably put your LED in backwards.) You will know this works because this blinks the LED twice as fast as the original program that is on your Arduino. If it blinks once a second, then you have not successfully sent your new program to the Arduino.

1.7 Comments

So far our programs have been only for the computer. But it turns out that you can put things in them that are only for the human readers. You can (and should) add comments to the program which the computer ignores and are for human readers only. This language supports two forms of comments:

1. The block comment style. It starts with a /* and continues until a */ is encountered. This can cross multiple lines. Below are three examples.

/* This is a comment */

/* So is this */

/* And * this * as * well */

2. A single line comment. It startswith a // and tells the computerto ignore the rest of the line.

// This is also a comment

Here is an example of what our earlier program might look like with com- ments added: (In this and all other code listings in this book, if a number doesn'tshow next to the line then it means it is a continuation of the line above but our paper isn't wide enough to show the entire thing. You will see an arrow at the end of the line that is to be continued and another arrow on the continuation line. That is just for this book, you will not see them in the IDE and you don't need to type them in.

Listing 1.3: Blink/Blink.pde

```
1 /* 2 * Program Name: Blink
```

1.8 Gotchas

```
3 * Author: Alan Smith 4 * Date Written:
17 March 2011 5 * Description: 6 * Turns
an LED on for one half second, then off for
one ← ! " → half second repeatedly. 7 */ 8
9 /* Pin Definitions */ 10 const int
kPinLed = 13;

11 12 /* 13 * Function Name: setup 14 *
Purpose: Run once when the system
powers up. 15 */ 16 void setup() 17 { 18
pinMode(kPinLed, OUTPUT); 19 }

20 21 /* 22 * Function name: loop 23 *
Purpose: Runs over and over again, as
long as the Arduino ← ! " → has power 24
*/ 25 void loop() 26 { 27
digitalWrite(kPinLed, HIGH); 28
delay(500); 29 digitalWrite(kPinLed,
LOW); 30 delay(500); 31 }
```

1.8 Gotchas

If your program won't compile (or it
doesn't do what you expect), here are a

few things to check that often confuse people:

Chapter 1 Getting Started

• The programming language is case sensitive. In other words, myVar is different than MyVar

• Whitespace (spaces, tabs, blank lines) is all collapsed tothe equivalent of a single space. It is for the human reader only.

• Blocks of code are encapsulated with curly braces ' {' and '}'

• Every open parenthesis'(' must have a matching close parenthesis ')'

• There are no commas in numbers. So you must say1000 and NOT 1,000.

• Each program statement needs to end with a semicolon';'. In general, this means that each line of your program will have a semicolon. Excep- tions are:

– Semicolons (like everything) are ignored in comments – Semicolons are not used after the end curly brace. '}'

1.9 Exercises

(There are sample solutions in AppendixC. However, you should struggle with them first and only look there when you are stuck. If you end up looking there, you should make up another exercise for yourself. The Challenge exercises do not have sample solutions.)

1. Change the amount of time the LED is off to 1 second. (Leaving the amount of time the LED is on at ½second.)

2. Change the pin to which the LED is connected from pin 13 to pin 2. (Note that both the circuit AND the program must be changed.)

3. Hook up 8 LEDs to pins 2 through 9 (with resistors, of course.) Modify the code to turn on each one in order and then extinguish them in order. - HINT: hook them up one additional LED at a time and make sure the new one works before you add the next one.

4. CHALLENGE: Now that you have 8 LEDs working, make them turn on and off in a pattern different from the one in exercise 3.

Chapter 2

Making Light Patterns

2.1 "Blinky"

In the last chapter, we made a light blink. Now let's look into ways to vary the pattern for a single LED. (Later in the chapter we'll hook up even more LEDs.) We will use the LED that is built into our Arduino on pin 13 for the first few sections in this chapter. (It is labeled "L" on the board and is on the left side behind the USB connector.)

2.2 IF Statements

So far all of our programs have executed all of the code. Control structures allow you to change which code is executed and even to execute code multiple times. The if statement is the first control structure. Here is an example of a program using it:

Listing 2.1: blink_if/blink_if.pde 1 const int kPinLed = 13;

2 3 void setup() 4 { 5 pinMode(kPinLed, OUTPUT); 6 }

7 8 int delayTime = 1000;

9 10 void loop() 11 { 12 delayTime = delayTime - 100; 13 if(delayTime <= 0){ // If the delay time is zero or ← !

" → less, reset it. 14 delayTime = 1000; 15 } 16 digitalWrite(kPinLed, HIGH); 17 delay(delayTime); 18 digitalWrite(kPinLed, LOW); 19 delay(delayTime); 20 }

Can you guess what this program will do? Let us go through it to make sure we all understandwhat it is doing and how to do similar things in our own programs. Lines 1 – 7 are identical to our first program. The first change is in line 8.

8 int delayTime = 1000;

Notice that this is similar to line 1 except there is no const keyword. That is because this is not a constant. It is a variable (which means its value can change or vary during the program.) We give it a start value of 1000. (Variables that are defined within a set of curly braces can only be used within those curly braces. They are called "local" variables. Variables that are defined outside a set of curly braces (like this one) are "global" and can be used everywhere.) Lines 9-11 are also identical to our first program, but then it starts to get very interesting.

12 delayTime = delayTime - 100;

Here we are changing the value of delay Time by subtracting 100 from its original value. Since the original value was 1000, after this happens the new value will be 900. Below are some of the math operators in the Arduino lan- guage.1

The Arduino language is very closely related to C++. For more details, go to http://www. arduino.cc

2.2 IF Statements

Operator2 Meaning = assignment operator + addition operator - subtraction operator * multiplication operator / division operator - be aware that if you are using integers only the whole part is kept. It is NOT rounded. For example: 5 / 2 == 2 % modulo operator - This gives the remainder. For example: 5 % 2 == 1 Next, we'll look at line 13-15:

13 if(delayTime <= 0){ // If the delay time is zero or ← !

```
"  → less, reset it. 14 delayTime = 1000; 15
}
```

The purpose of this section is to make sure the light always blinks. Since we are subtracting 100 from delayTime, we want to keep it from becoming 0 or negative. There are a number of comparison operators that we can use: Operator Meaning == is equal to != is not equal to < is less than > is greater than <= is less than or equal to >= is greater than or equal to In this case, we could have just tested for if(delayTime == 0) but since being negative is bad as well, we checked for it. In general, this is a good practice. (Imagine if we wanted to subtract 300 from delayTime instead of 100.) As you have probably figured out, if the delayTime is less than or equal to 0 then the delay time is set back to 1000.

I am not mentioning all of the operators here, just the more common ones. A full list is in Appendix A.

```
16   digitalWrite(kPinLed,   HIGH);   17
delay(delayTime);                     18
digitalWrite(kPinLed,      LOW);      19
delay(delayTime);
```

The remaining section turns the LED on and off. However, instead of using a fixed number, we use a variable so that we can change the delay time as the program runs. Pretty neat, huh?

2.3 ELSE Statements

And if statement can have an else clause which handles what should be done if the if statement isn't true. That sounds confusing, but here is an example:

Listing 2.2: blink_else/blink_else.pde 1 const int kPinLed = 13;

2 3 void setup() 4 { 5 pinMode(kPinLed, OUTPUT); 6 }

7 8 int delayTime = 1000;

9 10 void loop() 11 { 12 if(delayTime <= 100){ // If it is less than or equal to ← !

" → 100, reset it 13 delayTime = 1000; 14 } 15 else{ 16 delayTime = delayTime - 100; 17 } 18 digitalWrite(kPinLed, HIGH); 19   delay(delayTime);   20 digitalWrite(kPinLed,   LOW);   21 delay(delayTime);

2.4 WHILE statements

22 }

As you have probably guessed already, the code in line 13 is only done if the delayTime is less than or equal to 100. Otherwise, the code in line 16 is done, but NEVER both. Only one or the other is done. You may have noticed that instead of comparing to 0, like we did in section 2.2, that we compare to 100. This is because in this example we are comparing BEFORE we subtract 100 and in section 2.2, we compare AFTER. A question for thought: What would happen if we compared to 0 instead of 100?

2.4 WHILE statements

A while statement is just like an if statement except it continues to repeat a block of code (a block of code is what is within the curly braces.) as long as the condition is true. (and there is no else statement) Perhaps an example will make this more clear:

Listing 2.3: blink_while/blink_while.pde 1 const int kPinLed = 13;

2 3 void setup() 4 { 5 pinMode(kPinLed, OUTPUT); 6 }

7 8 int delayTime = 1000;

```
9 10 void loop() 11 { 12 while(delayTime
> 0){ // while delayTime is greater than 0
13    digitalWrite(kPinLed,  HIGH);    14
delay(delayTime);                      15
digitalWrite(kPinLed,     LOW);     16
delay(delayTime);   17    delayTime    =
delayTime - 100;

18 } 19 while(delayTime < 1000){ //
while delayTime is less than ← !

" → 1000 20 delayTime = delayTime +
100; // do this first so we don← !

" → 't have a loop with delayTime = 0 21
digitalWrite(kPinLed,     HIGH);    22
delay(delayTime);                      23
digitalWrite(kPinLed,     LOW);     24
delay(delayTime); 25 } 26 }
```

Can you figure out what this does?
Answer: It blinks faster, then slower.

2.5 What is truth(true)?

Ok, so there is something a little unusual
about this programming language (which
it shares with several others.) Rather than
define what true is, it defines what false is
and then defines everything as true that
isn't false. This seems strange, but it
works. FALSE is defined as zero (0).
Everything else is defined as true.

Sometimes you may come across code like this:

```
while (1){ digitalWrite(kPinLed, HIGH); delay(100); digitalWrite(kPinLed, LOW); delay(100); }
```

This will continue forever. 3 (Well, at least until you remove power or press the reset button on the Arduino.) One of the side effects of this is one of the most common programming mis- takes, accidentally using a = instead of a ==. Remember that a single equal

There is an advanced programming statement called break that will get you out of a loop like this, but we don't cover it in this book.

2.5 What is truth(true)?

sign= is an assignment (ie, it sets the variable to the value), and a double equals == is a test to see if they are the same. For example, imagine if we wanted a light to blink in a speeding up pattern and then repeat but accidentally used a single equals instead of a double equals. We might have some code like this:

```
int delayTime = 1000; void loop() {
if(delayTime = 0){ // BAD!!! should be ==
delayTime            =         1000;          }
digitalWrite(kPinLed,              HIGH);
delay(delayTime);   digitalWrite(kPinLed,
LOW);  delay(delayTime);  delayTime  =
delayTime - 100; }
```

This will assign 0 to delayTime. Theif statement will then check to see if 0 is true. It isn't (remember 0 is the definition of false.) So it doesn't exe- cute the delayTime = 1000, but every time through theloop() function delayTime will be 0. This isn't what we wanted to have happen at all!! For another example, imagine that we wanted the blinking to get less rapid and then reset but accidentally used a single equals instead of a double equals.

```
int delayTime = 100; void loop() {
if(delayTime = 1000){ // BAD!!! should be
==       delayTime       =       100;       }
digitalWrite(kPinLed,              HIGH);
delay(delayTime);   digitalWrite(kPinLed,
LOW);  delay(delayTime);  delayTime  =
delayTime + 100; }
```

Chapter 2 Making Light Patterns

In this case, it will assign 100 to delayTime. Theif statement will then check to see if 100 is true. It is (remember everything that isn't 0 is true). So ev- ery time it will assign 1000 to delayTimeand the blink rate will never change. Oops. These bugs can be difficult to track down so if you get something unusual look to make sure you didn't make this mistake.

2.6 Combinations

Sometimes you want to test for more than one thing. For example, you may want to test if a variable is between two numbers. While you can use multiple if statements, it is often more convenient and readable to use logical combi- nations. There are three ways that you can combine logical conditions. Operator Example Meaning && (A < 10) && (B > 5) logical AND (return TRUE if con- dition A AND condition B are true, otherwise return FALSE.) || (A < 10) || (B > 5) logical OR (return TRUE if condi- tion A OR condition B is true, oth- erwise return FALSE.) ! !(A < 10) logical NOT (return TRUE if con- dition A is false, otherwise return FALSE.) Something that isn't obvious is that youcan use the NOT operatoras a toggle for a variable that is intended to be either true or false(or LOW or HIGH). For example:

```
int ledState = LOW;

void loop() { ledState = !ledState; //
toggle        value        of        ledState
digitalWrite(kPinLed,              ledState);
delay(1000); }
```

2.7 FOR statements

In this case, ledState is LOW and then
when ledState = !ledState, it becomes
HIGH. On the next pass through the
loop,ledState is HIGH and when ledState =
!ledState it becomes LOW.

2.7 FOR statements

A for loop is the next control structure we
will be talking about. It is most useful
when you want something to happen
some number of times. Here is a simple
example.

Listing 2.4: blink_for/blink_for.pde 1
const int kPinLed = 13;

```
2 3 void setup() 4 { 5 pinMode(kPinLed,
OUTPUT); 6 }

7 8 void loop() 9 { 10 for(int i = 0; i < 4;
i++){ 11 digitalWrite(kPinLed, HIGH); 12
delay(200);    13    digitalWrite(kPinLed,
```

LOW);   14   delay(200);   15   }   16
delay(1000); // 1 second 17 }

There is something new in the for line
above. What is the i++? Well, it turns out
that programmers are a lazy bunch that
don't like to type more than necessary. So
they have come up with several shortcuts
for commonly done things. These are
called compound operators because they
combine the assign- ment operator with
another operator. All of the compound
operators are listed in Appendix A.1.8.
The two most common are:

Operator Meaning Example ++ increment
x++ means the same as x=x+1 --
decrement x-- means the same as x=x-1
The for statementhas three sub-
statements within it. It is composed like
the following:

for   (statement1;condition;statement2){
// statements }

Statement1 happens first and exactly
once. Each time through the loop, the
condition is tested; if it's true, the code
within the curly braces and then the
statement2 is executed. When the
condition is false, it goes to the code after
the statement block.

2.8 Our New Circuit

Ok, so now it is time to hook up more LEDs so we can do more exciting patterns.

1. Connect ground from the Arduino to the bottom row of the farthest right column.

2.8 Our New Circuit

2. Connect +5V from the Arduino to the bottom row of the next to right column. (This isn't actually necessary, but it is a good habit to always hook up the power and ground columns.)

3. LED1

a) Connect the resistor with one end in h2 and the other end on the far right column (ground). b) Connect an LED cathode (shorter leg) to f2. (This makes it connect to the resistor through the breadboard.) c) Connect same LED anode (longer leg) to f3. d) Connect j3 to pin 2 on the Arduino.

4. LED2

a) Connect another resistor with one end in h5 and the other end on the far right column (ground). b) Connect another LED cathode (shorter leg) to f5. c) Connect same LED anode (longer leg) to f6. d) Connect j6 to pin 3 on the Arduino.

5. LED3

a) Connect another resistor with one end in h8 and the other end on the far right column (ground). b) Connect another LED cathode (shorter leg) to f8. c) Connect same LED anode (longer leg) to f9. d) Connect j9 to pin 4 on the Arduino.

6. LED4

a) Connect another resistor with one end in h11 and the other end on the far right column (ground). b) Connect another LED cathode (shorter leg) to f11.

c) Connect same LED anode (longer leg) to f12. d) Connect j12 to pin 5 on the Arduino.

Now, lets try a program that will let us make sure that all of our hardware is made correctly. It is often wise to write a small piece of software to test and make sure your hardware is correct rather than try your full software on the brand new hardware. This code sets up LEDs on pins

2-5 and then cycles through turning each LED on and then off.

Listing 2.5: lightPattern1/lightPattern1.pde 1 const int kPinLed1 = 2; 2 const int kPinLed2 = 3; 3 const int kPinLed3 = 4; 4 const int kPinLed4 = 5;

5 6 void setup() 7 { 8 pinMode(kPinLed1, OUTPUT); 9 pinMode(kPinLed2, OUTPUT); 10 pinMode(kPinLed3, OUTPUT); 11 pinMode(kPinLed4, OUTPUT); 12 }

13 14 void loop() 15 { 16 // turn on each of the LEDs in order 17 digitalWrite(kPinLed1, HIGH); 18 delay(100); 19 digitalWrite(kPinLed2, HIGH); 20 delay(100); 21 digitalWrite(kPinLed3, HIGH); 22 delay(100); 23 digitalWrite(kPinLed4, HIGH); 24 delay(100);

25 26 // turn off each of the LEDs in order 27 digitalWrite(kPinLed1, LOW);

2.9 Introducing Arrays

28 delay(100); 29 digitalWrite(kPinLed2, LOW); 30 delay(100); 31

```
digitalWrite(kPinLed3,    LOW);    32
delay(100);   33   digitalWrite(kPinLed4,
LOW); 34 }
```

While this code works just fine, it isn't
very elegant and it seems like there is a
lot of writing of very similar things and
opportunities for mistakes. Let's see how
we can do a better job.

2.9 Introducing Arrays

An array is a collection of variables that
are indexed with an index number. An
example will help us to understand.

Listing   2.6:
lightPattern1b/lightPattern1b.pde   1
const int k_numLEDs = 4; 2 const int
kPinLeds[k_numLEDs] = {2,3,4,5}; //
LEDs connected← !

" → to pins 2-5

3 4 void setup() 5 { 6 for(int i = 0; i <
k_numLEDs; i++){ 7 pinMode(kPinLeds[i],
OUTPUT); 8 } 9 }

10 11 void loop() 12 { 13 for(int i = 0; i <
k_numLEDs;   i++){   14
digitalWrite(kPinLeds[i],   HIGH);   15
delay(100); 16 } 17 for(int i = k_numLEDs
- 1; i >= 0; i--){

18 digitalWrite(kPinLeds[i], LOW); 19 delay(100); 20 } 21 }

Can you figure out what this does? If not, don't panic. We are going to go through this code and look at each part.

1 const int k_numLEDs = 4;

First, we define how many elements are going to be in our array. We use this later to make sure that we don't try to read (or write) past the end of our array. (Arduino does not stopyou from doing this which can cause all sortsofstrange problems.)

2 const int kPinLeds[k_numLEDs] = {2,3,4,5}; // LEDs connected← !

" → to pins 2-5

Second, we define the array. You'll notice that we have the number of "ele- ments" in the array in brackets. We could have used the actual number, but it is much better to use a constant. We assign the values to the array here. The values are inside of curly braces and are separated by commas. Arrays are zero-indexed, which can be confusing. That means the first element in the array k_LEDPinsis k_LEDPins[0]. The last element in the array is k_LEDPins[3]. (0-3 is 4 elements.)

4 void setup() 5 { 6 for(int i = 0; i < k_numLEDs; i++){ 7 pinMode(kPinLeds[i], OUTPUT); 8 } 9 }

Here we use a for loop to go through each of the elements in our array and setthemas OUTPUT.Toaccess each elementin thearray, we usesquare brackets with the index inside. 4 4Some of you may be wondering if we could have just used pins 2-5 without using an array. Yes, we could have. But you don't want to. If in a later circuit you decide to use pins that aren't next to each other the array method works, and the other one doesn't.

2.10 Exercises

13 for(int i = 0; i < k_numLEDs; i++){ 14 digitalWrite(kPinLeds[i], HIGH); 15 delay(100); 16 }

This looks almost exactly the same as what is done in setup. Here we are going through each of the LEDs and turning them on (with a 100 millisecond delay in between them).

17 for(int i = k_numLEDs - 1; i >= 0; i--){ 18 digitalWrite(kPinLeds[i], LOW); 19 delay(100); 20 }

Now we are showing that we can use a for loop to go backwards through the loop as well. We start at k_numLEDs - 1 since arrays are zero-indexed. If we started at k_LEDPins[4], that would be past the end of our array. We check >= 0 since we don't want to miss the first element (the one at index 0.)

2.10 Exercises

1. Modify the blink_for program in Section 2.7 to light the LED up 10 times in a row instead of 4.

2. Make a program (sketch) that lights up a single LED five times in a row for one second on and off, and then five times in a row for ½of a second on and off.

3. Make a program using arrays that lights up the LEDs from top to bottom and then goes backwards so only one LED is on at any time. (This is often called a "Cylon"5 or a "Larson"6 light.)

4. Make a program that lights up the LEDs in any pattern that you like.

5from Battlestar Galactica 6the producer of Knight Rider

Chapter 3

Input

Until now, we have only used the Arduino to control other things. It is time for us to start sensing the real world! After we do this, then our Arduino will be able to make decisions of what to do based off of input from the outside world. In this chapter we will start with a simple circuit and continue to add pieces to it.

3.1 Pushbuttons

What is a pushbutton? Pushing a button causes wires under the button to be connected, allowing current to flow. (called closed) When the button isn't pressed, no current can flow because the wires aren't touching (called open) . 1

The symbol for a push button may be helpful here. You can tell that pushing down on the top causes there to be a connection, and a spring causes it to not be connected when it isn't being pushed down.

1This is true for the most common type of push button called "normally open" (often abbreviated NO). There is a less common type called "normally closed" (abbreviated NC) that is closed (connected) when not pushed and open when pushed.

3.1.1 One button and an LED

3.1.1.1 Circuit

1. Connect the far right column (Ground) on the breadboard to GND on the Arduino.

2. Connect the next to right column (+) to 5V on the Arduino.

3. Put the pushbutton legs in e5, e7, f5, and f7. (If they won't fit in these squares, turn the switch 90º (¼of a turn) and try again.)

4. Connect h7 to the pin 2 on the Arduino.

5. Connect h5 to the far right column (ground).

6. Connect a 330Ω (orange-orange-brown) resistor with one end in h2 and

the other end on the far right column (ground).

7. Connect the LED cathode (shorter leg) to f2. (This makes it connect to the resistor through the breadboard.)

8. Connect the LED anode (longer leg) to f3.

9. Connect h3 to pin 9 on the Arduino.

3.1 Pushbuttons

The push buttons have four legs. When the button is pressed it connects the two legs on the right side together. (It also connects the two on the left, but we aren't using those now.)

3.1.1.2 Programming

Let us start with some sample code and see if you can guess what it does.

Listing 3.1: button1/button1.pde 1 const int kPinButton1 = 2; 2 const int kPinLed = 9;

3 4 void setup() 5 { 6 pinMode(kPinButton1, INPUT); 7

digitalWrite(kPinButton1, HIGH); // turn on pull-up ← !

" → resistor 8 pinMode(kPinLed, OUTPUT); 9 }

10 11 void loop() 12 { 13 if(digitalRead(kPinButton1) == LOW){ 14 digitalWrite(kPinLed, HIGH); 15 } 16 else{ 17 digitalWrite(kPinLed, LOW); 18 } 19 }

Can you guess? There are a number of things here that seem unusual, so let's talk about them.

4 void setup() 5 { 6 pinMode(kPinButton1, INPUT);

2Switches are rated by how much current and voltage can go through them. So don't try to replace the light switches in your house with these little buttons!

7 digitalWrite(kPinButton1, HIGH); // turn on pull-up ← !

" → resistor 8 pinMode(kPinLed, OUTPUT); 9 }

First, we setup the buttonPin as INPUT. That is pretty straightforward. Next, we write HIGH to the INPUT pin. Wait a second, how are we writing something to input?? Well, this is an unusual aspect to the Arduino. Writing HIGH to an input turns on an internal 20kΩ pull-up resistor. (Writing LOW to an input pin turns it off.) The next obvious question should be "ok, what is a pull-up resistor?" For electricity to flow, there has to be a complete circuit from the power to the ground. If a micro-controller pin is not connected to anything, it is said to be "floating" and you can't know ahead of time what the value will be when you read it. It can also change between times that it is read. When we add a pull-up resistor, we get a circuit like the following:

When a pushbutton is pushed down, the circuit is complete and ground is connectedto pin 2. (The +5V goesthroughthe closed switch to ground as well.) When it is notpushed downthe circuit is from the +5V throughtheresistorand the micro-controller sees the +5V. (HIGH) Itturnsoutthatthisissocommonlyneededth atthedesignersoftheArduino put a resistor inside that you can use by writing some code. Isn't that neat? Next, we look at our main loop:

3.1 Pushbuttons

```
11    void    loop()    12    {    13
if(digitalRead(kPinButton1) == LOW){ 14
digitalWrite(kPinLed, HIGH); 15 } 16 else{
17 digitalWrite(kPinLed, LOW); 18 } 19 }
```

If the button is pressed, then the pin will be connected to ground (which we will see as LOW). If it isn't pressed, the pull-up resistor will have it internally connected to +5V (which we will see as HIGH.) Since we want the LED to light when the button is pressed, we write HIGH out when the value read from the pin connected to the button is LOW. A few intermediate exercises:

1. Try this program and make sure it works. (If it doesn't, rotate the button 90 degrees and try again.)

2. Change it so the LED is normally on and pressing the button turns it off

3.1.2 Two buttons and an LED

Ok,so we could have done the last circuit without a micro-controller at all. (Can you figure out how to modify the first circuit in this book with a pushbutton to do the same thing?) Now, lets do something a little more exciting. Let us make a circuit where we can change the brightness of an LED. So far, we have either had the LED on (HIGH) or off (LOW). How do we change the brightness of an LED? It turns out there are two ways.

1. Change the amount of current going through the LED. (We could do this by changing the size of the resistor.)

2. Take advantage of the fact that people can only see things that happen up to a certain speed, and turn the LED on and off faster than we can see. The more time that the LED is on in a given period of time, the "brighter" we think it is. The more time it is off, the "dimmer" we think it is. (This method supports smoother dimming over a broader range as opposed to changing resistors.)

It turns out that this method of turning things on and off quickly is very common, and a standard method has been designed called Pulse Width Modulation (PWM for short). The Arduino supports PWM (on certain pins marked with a tilde(~) on your board - pins 3, 4,5,9,10 and 11) at 500Hz. (500 times a second.) You can give it a value between 0 and 255. 0 means that it is never 5V. 255 meansit is always 5V. To do this you make a call to analogWrite()with the value. The ratio of "ON" time to total time is called the "duty cycle". A PWM output that is ON half the time is said to have a duty cycle of 50%. Below is an example showing what the pulses look like:

3.1 Pushbuttons

You can think of PWM as being on for x 255where x is the value you send with analogWrite().

3.1.2.1 Circuit

Enough talking! Let's make something! First, let us add to our circuit.

1. Place a second pushbutton in e9,e11,f9 and f11.

2. Connect h9 to the far left column (ground).

3. Connect h11 to pin 3 of the Arduino.

(You can test to make sure you have the button put in correctly by connecting h11 to pin 2 instead of the first button and making sure it works before you upload a new program to the Arduino.)

3.1.2.2 Programming

Here is a sample program that uses a button to dim the LED and another button to increase the brightness:

Listing 3.2: button2/button2.pde 1 const int kPinButton1 = 2;

Chapter 3 Input

2 const int kPinButton2 = 3; 3 const int kPinLed = 9;

```
4   5   void   setup()   6   {   7
pinMode(kPinButton1,   INPUT);   8
pinMode(kPinButton2,   INPUT);   9
pinMode(kPinLed,   OUTPUT);   10
digitalWrite(kPinButton1, HIGH); // turn
on   pullup   resistor   11
```

digitalWrite(kPinButton2, HIGH); // turn on pullup resistor 12 }

13 14 int ledBrightness = 128; 15 void loop()   16   {   17 if(digitalRead(kPinButton1) == LOW){ 18 ledBrightness--;   19   }   20   else if(digitalRead(kPinButton2) == LOW){ 21 ledBrightness++; 22 }

23   24   ledBrightness   = constrain(ledBrightness,   0,   255);   25 analogWrite(kPinLed, ledBrightness); 26 delay(20); 27 }

There are 3 lines that may need a little explaining

24   ledBrightness   = constrain(ledBrightness,   0,   255);   25 analogWrite(kPinLed, ledBrightness); 26 delay(20);

Line24 demonstrates a new built-in function that is very useful called constrain(). The function contains code similar to this:

Listing 3.3: Constrain int constrain(int value, int min, int max) {

3.2 Potentiometers

```
if(value > max){ value = max; } if(value <
min){ value = min; } return value;

}
```

The functions we have written before all started with void, meaning they didn't return anything. This function starts with int meaning it returns an integer. (We will talk more about different types of variables later. For now, just remember that an integer has no fractional part.) Ok, so what this means is line 24 guarantees the value of ledBrightness will be between 0 and 255 (including 0 and 255). Line 25 uses analogWrite to tell Arduino to perform PWM on that pin with the set value. Line 26 delays for 20 milliseconds so that we won't make adjustments faster than 50 times in a second. (You can adjust this to find where you think the best response is to your pressing the buttons.) The reason we do this is that people are much slower than the Arduino. If we didn't do this, then this program would appear that pressing the first button turns the LED off and pressing the second button turns it on (Try it and see!)

CHALLENGE question - What happens if both pushbuttons are pressed? Why?

3.2 Potentiometers

We used pushbuttons for digital input in the last section. Now let's look at using a potentiometer. (A potentiometer is a resistor whose value changes smoothly as it is turned. This is used often as an adjustment "knob" in many electronics.)

3.2.1 Circuit

The potentiometer has three legs. The one in the middle should be connected to ANALOG IN 0 on the Arduino. One of the sides should be connected to +5V and the other to GND. (ground). (If you get these backwards then your potentiometer will work in the backwards direction of what you expect.) Digital means something is either on or off. Analog means it can have a continuous range of values. The Arduino has some built-in "analog inputs" that convert the voltage seen on the pin to a number that we can use in our programs. (They return between 0 and 1023. So, 0V would read as 0 and 5V would read as 1023.)

1. Place the potentiometer (often called "pot" for short) in f13, f14, and f15.

2. Connect j13 to the next to right most column (+5V).

3. Connect j15 to the right most column (ground).

4. Connect j14 to the A0 pin (Analog In 0) on the Arduino.

3.2.2 Programming

Listing 3.4: pot1/pot1.pde 1 const int kPinPot = A0; 2 const int kPinLed = 9;

3.2 Potentiometers

3 4 void setup() 5 { 6 pinMode(kPinPot, INPUT); 7 pinMode(kPinLed, OUTPUT); 8 }

9 10 void loop() 11 { 12 int ledBrightness; 13 int sensorValue = 0;

14   15   sensorValue   = analogRead(kPinPot); 16 ledBrightness = map(sensorValue, 0, 1023, 0, 255);

17   18   analogWrite(kPinLed, ledBrightness); 19 }

There are two things here that are different from anything we have done before.

1. The constant k_PotPin is defined as A0. (The A is a shortcut to mean it is one of the analog pins.)3

2. Line 16 demonstrates a new built-in function that is very useful called map(). This function re-maps a number from one range to the other. It is called like map(value, fromLow, fromHigh, toLow, toHigh). This is useful because the analogReadreturns a value in the range of 0-1023. But analogWrite can only take a value from 0-255. 4

Since you can affect the brightness of an LED by varying the resistance, we could have just used the potentiometer as a variable resistor in the circuit. So

Shhh, don't tell anyone but actually means pin 14. A1 means pin 15, and so on. And you can actually use them as digital inputs and outputs if you run out of those pins. But you can't use digital pins as analog inputs. I recommend using the A# for the analog pins so it is obvious what you are doing. This maps linearly. So something that is halfway in the From range will return the value that is halfway in the To range.

Now let us do something we can't do easily without a micro-controller. This next program changes how quickly the LED blinks based off of the value read from the potentiometer.

Listing 3.5: pot2/pot2.pde 1 const int kPinPot = A0; 2 const int kPinLed = 9;

3 4 void setup() 5 { 6 pinMode(kPinLed, OUTPUT); 7 }

8 9 void loop() 10 { 11 int sensorValue;

12   13   sensorValue   = analogRead(kPinPot);

14 15 digitalWrite(kPinLed, HIGH); 16 delay(sensorValue);   17 digitalWrite(kPinLed,   LOW);   18 delay(sensorValue); 19 }

3.2.3 A way to avoid delay()

The program in the last section was pretty neat, but the light has to go through a full cycle of on and off before it checks the potentiometer again. So when the delay is long it takes it a long time to notice that we have changed the potentiometer. With some tricky programming, we can check the value more often and not wait until the full delay time was used up. Let's see an example.

Listing 3.6: pot3/pot3.pde 1 const int kPinPot = A0; 2 const int kPinLed = 9;

3

3.2 Potentiometers

4 void setup() 5 { 6 pinMode(kPinLed, OUTPUT); 7 }

8 9 long lastTime = 0; 10 int ledValue = LOW;

11 12 void loop() 13 { 14 int sensorValue;

15   16   sensorValue   = analogRead(kPinPot); 17 if(millis() > lastTime + sensorValue){ 18 if(ledValue == LOW){ 19 ledValue = HIGH; 20 } 21 else{ 22 ledValue = LOW; 23 } 24 lastTime = millis(); 25 digitalWrite(kPinLed, ledValue); 26 } 27 }

Let's talk about some things that are different.

9 long lastTime = 0;

So far we have only used a variable type called int. It turns out that there are several different types of variables you can have. Here they are:

Type contains boolean can contain either true or false char -128 to 127 unsigned char 0 to 255 byte (same as unsigned char) int -32,768 to 32,767 unsigned int 0 to 65,535 word (same as unsigned int) long (or long int) -2,147,483,648 to 2,147,483,647 unsigned long 0 to 4,294,967,295 float -3.4028235E+38 to 3.4028235E+38 double (same as float) The only thing you need to know about this now is that if you are trying to store a number that may be too big to fit into an int, you can use along (or a long int). (This table is true for Arduino, but can vary from computer to computer.) The second new thing is that we are using a new function called millis(). This returns the number of milliseconds the Arduino has been running since it started last.5 This function returns a long since if it returned an int, it wouldn't be able to count very long. Can you figure out how long? (Answer: 32.767 seconds) So instead of using delay(), we keep checkingmillis()

and when the appropriate number of milliseconds has passed, then we change the LED. We then store the last time we changed in the lastTime variable so we can check again at the right time.

3.3 RGB LEDs

Up until this point, we have used LEDs that are only a single color. We could change the color by changing the LED. Wouldn't it be cool if we could choose any color we wanted? What about teal, purple, orange, or even more???

It will actually "rollover" and start counting over again after about 50 days from when it is zero. But that is long enough it won't be important to you for this class.

3.3 RGB LEDs

Introducing our new friend, the RGB LED. An RGB LED is really three small LEDs next to each other. A Red one, a Green one, and a Blue one. (Hence, why it is called RGB). It turns out that you can make any color by mixing these three light colors together. You use the same PWM method we discussed earlier in the chapter for each part of the red, the green, and the blue. Let's hook it up with three potentiome- ters so we can vary each one and it should make more sense.

3.3.1 Circuit

This may look a lot more complicated, but it is all a repeat of other things you have done. You CAN do it!!!

1. Put a second Pot in f17, f18, f19. (The blue pots we are using for the class will be touching. This is ok.)

2. Connect j17 to the next to right most column (+5V).

3. Connect j19 to the right most column (ground).

4. Connect j18 to the A1 pin on the Arduino.

5. Put the third Pot in f21, f22, f23.

6. Connect j21 to the next to right most column (+5V).

7. Connect j23 to the right most column (ground).

8. Connect j22 to the A2 pin on the Arduino.

9. Put the RGB LED (you can tell it because it's the one with four legs) in f26, f27, f28, f29 with the cathode (longest leg) in f27. (this should be the leg second from the top.)

10. Put a resistor from h27 to the far right column (ground).

11. Connect h26 to pin 6 on the Arduino.

12. Connect h28 to pin 10 on the Arduino.

13. Connect h29 to pin 11 on the Arduino.

3.3.2 Programming

Following is a program that will let us control the color of the LED by turning 3 different potentiometers. One will be read for the value ofRed, one for the value of Green, and one for the value of Blue.

Listing 3.7: rgb_3pot/rgb_3pot.pde 1 const int kPinPot1 = A0; 2 const int kPinPot2 = A1; 3 const int kPinPot3 = A2; 4 const int kPinLed_R = 6; 5 const int kPinLed_G = 10; 6 const int kPinLed_B = 11;

```
7  8  void  setup()  9  {  10
pinMode(kPinLed_R,    OUTPUT);    11
pinMode(kPinLed_G,    OUTPUT);    12
pinMode(kPinLed_B, OUTPUT); 13 }

14 15 void loop() 16 {
```

3.4 Exercises

```
17 int potValue; 18 int ledValue;

19 20 potValue = analogRead(kPinPot1);
21 ledValue = map(potValue, 0, 1023, 0,
255);     22     analogWrite(kPinLed_R,
ledValue);

23 24 potValue = analogRead(kPinPot2);
25 ledValue = map(potValue, 0, 1023, 0,
255);     26     analogWrite(kPinLed_G,
ledValue);

27 28 potValue = analogRead(kPinPot3);
29 ledValue = map(potValue, 0, 1023, 0,
255);     30     analogWrite(kPinLed_B,
ledValue); 31 }
```

You may notice that when you turn all of the pots to full on that instead of white you get red. The reason for this is that the red LED is stronger than the other two. You can experiment with the values in the map() function before sending it to the red part of the LED so that it will be more balanced.

3.4 Exercises

1. Make the two push buttons a "gas" and "brake" button. The "gas"button should speed up the blinking rate of the LED, and the "brake" button should slow it down.

2. Change the speed at which the LED blinks based off of the value of the pot ONLY when the first button is pressed. (In other words, you can adjust the potentiometer, but it has no effect until you press the "ON" button)

3. CHALLENGE: Use the two buttons to store a "from" and a "to" color. When neither buttonis pressed,the RGB LED should fade smoothly from one color to the other and back.

4. CHALLENGE:Can youfind outhowlong it is betweenthe last statement in the loop() function and the first one?

Chapter 4

Sound

So far we have just been playing with lights. In this chapter, we will add making simple sounds and music. In order to make a sound, we turn the speaker on and off a certain number of times per second. Specifically, middle A (a musical note) is 440 Hz. (Hz is short for and is pronounced "Hertz" - the number of times (or cycles) per second.) So all we need to do to play a middle A is to make a sound wave that cycles 440 times per second. We will approximate the sine wave with a square wave (those terms just describe the shape). In order to calculate how much time we need to have the speaker on for: timeDelay = 1 second 2* toneFrequency. This has a 2 in the denominator because half of the time is with the speaker on and half is with the speaker off. timeDelay = 1 second 2* 440 timeDelay = 1136 microSeconds (a microsecond is 1 1,000,000th of a second.)

4.1 Our Circuit

First, let's hook up the speaker to pin 9. (The other pin of the speaker simply goes to ground.)

1. Connect the far right column (Ground) to GND on the Arduino.

2. Connect the next to right column (+) to 5V on the Arduino,

3. Connect the black wire of the speaker to the far right column (ground).

4. Connect the red wire of the speaker to pin 9 on the Arduino.

HINT: If the speaker is too loud,simply put a 330Ω resistor in between the speaker and pin 9 of the Arduino.

4.2 Simple note

We talked about the delay() function before. (Remember the units are in milliseconds or 1 1000th of a second.) There is also a delayMicroseconds() function (a microsecond is 1 1,000,000th of a second.) So all we need to do is set up our speaker pin, and then raise and lower the voltage on that pin 440 times a second. Remember at the beginning of this chapter where we figured out that we need to have the speaker on (and then off) for 1136 microseconds. Run this program and you should hear an A (musical note) that will not stop (until you pull power.)

Listing 4.1: sound_simple/sound_simple.pde 1 const int kPinSpeaker = 9;

4.3 Music

```
2 const int k_timeDelay = 1136;

3 4 void setup() 5 { 6 pinMode(kPinSpeaker, OUTPUT); 7 }

8 9 void loop() 10 { 11 digitalWrite(kPinSpeaker, HIGH); 12 delayMicroseconds(k_timeDelay); 13 digitalWrite(kPinSpeaker, LOW); 14 delayMicroseconds(k_timeDelay); 15 }
```

4.3 Music

Now that we can make a simple note, we can make music. It turns out that the Arduino has 2 functions built-in that handle making sounds as well. The first is tone()which takes2 required parameters(and an optional third). tone(pin, frequency, duration) OR tone(pin, frequency) These both return right away, regardless of the duration you give it. If you don't include a duration, the sound will play until you call tone() again or until you call noTone(). (This may require you using a delay function if playing a tone is the main thing you are doing.) The duration is in milliseconds. The reason the duration is useful is that you can give it an amount of time to play and then you can go and do other things. When the duration is over it will stop. The second is noTone() which takes a single parameter: noTone(pin) It basically stops whatever tone is playing on that pin.

(A strange warning. When the tone() function is running, PWM (pulse width modulation that we used in section 3.1.2) won't run on pin 3 and pin 11. So if you are using a speaker in your sketch, you might want to avoid using those pins as PWM entirely.)1 You may hook a speaker up to any of the pins. Here is an example to try on your Arduino: (Ok, so it is a simple C scale and probably not really music.)

Listing 4.2: sound_2/sound_2.pde 1 #define NOTE_C4 262 2 #define NOTE_D4 294 3 #define NOTE_E4 330 4 #define

NOTE_F4 349 5 #define NOTE_G4 392 6 #define NOTE_A4 440 7 #define NOTE_B4 494 8 #define NOTE_C5 523

9 10 const int kPinSpeaker = 9;

11 12 void setup() 13 { 14 pinMode(kPinSpeaker, OUTPUT); 15 }

16 17 void loop() 18 { 19 tone(kPinSpeaker, NOTE_C4, 500); 20 delay(500); 21 tone(kPinSpeaker, NOTE_D4, 500); 22 delay(500); 23 tone(kPinSpeaker, NOTE_E4, 500); 24 delay(500); 25 tone(kPinSpeaker, NOTE_F4, 500); 26 delay(500); 27 tone(kPinSpeaker, NOTE_G4, 500);

1I know you are probably curious about this really strange limitation. The details are beyond the scope of this book, so just remember the strange limitation.

4.4 Music with functions

28 delay(500); 29 tone(kPinSpeaker, NOTE_A4, 500); 30 delay(500); 31 tone(kPinSpeaker, NOTE_B4, 500); 32 delay(500); 33 tone(kPinSpeaker, NOTE_C5, 500); 34 delay(500);

35 36 noTone(kPinSpeaker);

37 38 delay(2000); 39 }

The only thing here you haven't seen before is #define. #define is a search and replace command to the computer during compilation. Any time it finds the first thing (up to a space), it replaces it with the rest of the line.2 So in this example, when the computer finds NOTE_E4, it replaces it with a value of 330. We won't talk here about how to determine what the frequency is of each note. However, there is a file on your USB stick called pitches.h that has all of the frequencies for all of the notes on a piano keyboard. This file is also available from http://www.introtoarduino.com.

4.4 Music with functions

It seems like there ought to be someway to reduce all of the repetition above. Up until this point, we have only used the two required functions or functions that come with the Arduino. It is time for us to create our own function! Every function starts with what type of variable it returns. (void is a certain type that means it doesn't return anything.) (Remember there is a list of variable types in Section

3.2.3.) It then has the function name (how it is called), an open parenthesis "(" and then a list of parameters separated by commas. Each parameter has a variable type followed by a name. Then it has a close parenthesis ")". The parameters

These are called macros and you can actually do more powerful things with them but that is outside the scope of this book. If you are interested, do some searching on the Internet.

It can be used within the function as variables. As an example, we'll create a function called ourTone() that will combine the tone() and delay() lines so that the function won't return until the note is done playing.

Listing 4.3: sound_3/sound_3.pde 1 #define NOTE_C4 262 2 #define NOTE_D4 294 3 #define NOTE_E4 330 4 #define NOTE_F4 349 5 #define NOTE_G4 392 6 #define NOTE_A4 440 7 #define NOTE_B4 494 8 #define NOTE_C5 523

9 10 const int kPinSpeaker = 9;

11 12 void setup() 13 { 14 pinMode(kPinSpeaker, OUTPUT); 15 }

```
16
17 void loop() 18 {
19 ourTone(NOTE_C4, 500);
20 ourTone(NOTE_D4, 500);
21 ourTone(NOTE_E4, 500);
22 ourTone(NOTE_F4, 500);
23 ourTone(NOTE_G4, 500);
24 ourTone(NOTE_A4, 500);
25 ourTone(NOTE_B4, 500);
26 ourTone(NOTE_C5, 500);
27
28 noTone(kPinSpeaker);
29 delay(2000); 30 }
31
32 void ourTone(int freq, int duration)
33 {
```

4.4 Music with functions

```
34 tone(kPinSpeaker, freq, duration); 35
delay(duration); 36 }
```

Functions can be a huge help in making your program easier to understand. Here is an example so we can now specify what we want to play in two arrays (one that holds the notes, and one that holds the beats.)

Listing 4.4: sound_array/sound_array.pde
```
1 #include "pitches.h"
```

```
2 3 int kPinSpeaker = 9;

4 5 #define NUM_NOTES 15

6 7 const int notes[NUM_NOTES] = // a 0 represents a rest 8 { 9 NOTE_C4, NOTE_C4, NOTE_G4, NOTE_G4, 10 NOTE_A4, NOTE_A4, NOTE_G4, NOTE_F4, 11 NOTE_F4, NOTE_E4, NOTE_E4, NOTE_D4, 12 NOTE_D4, NOTE_C4, 0 13 };

14 15 const int beats[NUM_NOTES] = { 16 1, 1, 1, 1, 1, 1, 2, 1, 1, 1, 1, 1, 1, 2, 4 }; 17 const int beat_length = 300;

18 19 void setup() 20 { 21 pinMode(kPinSpeaker, OUTPUT); 22 }

23 24 void loop() 25 { 26 for (int i = 0; i < NUM_NOTES; i++) { 27 if (notes[i] == 0) { 28 delay(beats[i] * beat_length); // rest 29 } 30 else {


31 ourTone(notes[i], beats[i] * beat_length); 32 } 33 // pause between notes 34 noTone(kPinSpeaker); 35 delay(beat_length / 2); 36 } 37 }

38 39 void ourTone(int freq, int duration) 40 { 41 tone(kPinSpeaker, freq, duration); 42 delay(duration); 43 }
```

In line 1, you'll see the #include statement. What this does is take the entire file within the quotes and put it where the #include statement is. By convention, these are almost always placed at the top of a program.

4.5 Exercises

1. Make a sketch that plays the first line of "Happy Birthday"

a) C4 (1 beat), C4 (1 beat), D4 (2 beats), C4 (2 beats), F4 (2 beats), E4 (4 beats)

2. Add 2 buttons to the circuit. For a reminder of how to hookup and program buttons, see section 3.1. When you press each button have it play a different tune.

3. Change ourTone() to not use the tone() and noTone() functions. (HINT: use the technique shown in section 4.2.)

Chapter 5

Making a digital thermometer

Before we start on the fun work of making a digital thermometer, we are going to take a slight detour in the next section so that we can test out parts of our program before putting it all together. Writing small parts of your program and making sure it works before doing more is wise as it makes tracking down problems much much easier.

5.1 Serial Monitor

Until this point when our programs (sketches) didn't work, we just pulled out our hair and tried harder. Perhaps some of you put in an extra LED and turned it on and off at certain points in your program so that you would know what your program was doing. Well, now we will learn a much easier way. Built into the Arduino platform is an ability to talk back to the user's computer. You may have noticed that Pins 0 and 1 on the Arduino say "RX" and "TX" next to them. These pins are monitored by another chip on the Arduino that converts these pins to go over the USB cable (if it is plugged in both to your Arduino and the computer.) I have the entire program below first. Read through it, but we will explain the new parts after the sample program. This program is the same as the one in section 2.2 except it has some extra code in it to help us see what the program is doing.

Listing 5.1: blink_if_serial/blink_if_serial.pde 1 const int kPinLed = 13;

2

3 void setup() 4 { 5 pinMode(kPinLed, OUTPUT); 6 Serial.begin(9600); 7 }

8 9 int delayTime = 1000;

10 11 void loop() 12 { 13 delayTime = delayTime - 100; 14 if(delayTime <= 0){ // If it would have been zero or ← !

" → less, reset it. 15 delayTime = 1000; 16 } 17 Serial.print("delayTime = "); 18 Serial.println(delayTime); 19 digitalWrite(kPinLed, HIGH); 20 delay(delayTime); 21 digitalWrite(kPinLed, LOW); 22 delay(delayTime); 23 }

You'll notice a couple of new things. First, there is a new line in the setup() function.

6 Serial.begin(9600);

This basically says that we want to use the Serial1 code and to start it at 9600 baud.2 This number and the one in the serial monitor (described later) MUST match or you will see gibberish in the serial monitor. (9600 is the default, so it is easiest to use that.) The second new thing is in lines 17-18.

17 Serial.print("delayTime = "); 18 Serial.println(delayTime);

1Serial means that it is sent one bit after another. 2Baud is how many bits per second are transmitted.

5.1 Serial Monitor

The only difference between Serial.print and Serial.println is that Serial.println means that the next thing sent out the serial port after this one will start on the next line. There is a third new thing you may have noticed. There is something in quotes ("). This is called a string. In this book we will only use strings as constants.3 Upload and run it. Hmm, it seems like the LED just blinked and nothing else new happened (except now we see the TX light blink on the board. That is because we don't have the Serial Monitor window up.

Open the Serial Monitor by clicking on the Serial Monitor box in the IDE. It should look like the screenshot below. Make SURE the baud (speed) is set to 9600. It is located in the bottom right corner. (The important thing is that it is set the same in our program and here. Since the default here is 9600, we set our program to that to minimize our needing to change settings.) If you have the baud set differently, you will see garbage instead of what you expect.

3A string is really an array of bytes. But a full discussion of strings is outside the scope of this book.

Before going any further, make sure that when you run your program you see the lines "delayTime = " with the value of delayTime on the Serial Monitor.

5.2 Measuring the temperature

We are using a chip called TMP36. It can report the temperature from -40 degrees Celsius to 150 degrees Celsius (or -40 degrees Fahrenheit to 302 degrees Fahrenheit.) Accuracy decreasesafter 125 degreesCelsius, but since water boils at 100 degrees Celsius that is ok.

1. Connect the far right column to ground (GND) on the Arduino.

2. Connect the next to right column to +5V.

3. Put pin 1 of the TMP36 in f1. (The curved part of the temperature sensor should face the left edge of the breadboard. If you get this backwards, it will heat up and can burn you.)

4. Connect j1 to the far right column (GND).

5. Connect j3 to the next to right column (+5V).

6. Connect j2 to A0 on the Arduino.

Now here is the code that will read the temperature sensor and send the values to the serial monitor on the computer. Again, we will show the entire code first and then go through the new sections afterwards.

Listing 5.2: temp_serial/temp_serial.pde 1 const int kPinTemp = A0;

```
2 3 void setup() 4 { 5 Serial.begin(9600);
6 }

7 8 void loop() 9 { 10 float temperatureC
= getTemperatureC();

11  12  Serial.print(temperatureC);  13
Serial.println(" degrees C");

14 15 // now convert to Fahrenheit 16
float          temperatureF          =
convertToF(temperatureC);

17  18  Serial.print(temperatureF);  19
Serial.println(" degrees F");

20 21 delay(500); 22 }



23 24 float getTemperatureC() 25 { 26 int
reading = analogRead(kPinTemp);

27 28 float voltage = (reading * 5.0) /
1024; 29 // convert from 10 mv per
degree with 500mV offset 30 // to
degrees ((voltage - 500mV) * 100) 31
return (voltage - 0.5) * 100; 32 }
```

33   34   float   convertToF(float temperatureC)   35   {   36   return (temperatureC * 9.0 / 5.0) + 32.0; 37 }

So we'll start near the very beginning of loop.   10   float   temperatureC   = getTemperatureC();

You will notice that we use the float variable type. This variable type is the only one that allows you to store anything other than integer numbers (number with no decimal or fractional part.) Floats are only accurate to about 6-7 digits. This is important only because you can end up with rounding er- rors when using them. So when doing comparisons, make sure that you are checking to see if they are "close" instead of equal. We call our own function getTemperatureC().   24   float getTemperatureC() 25 { 26 int reading = analogRead(kPinTemp);

27 28 float voltage = (reading * 5.0) / 1024; 29 // convert from 10 mv per degree with 500mV offset 30 // to degrees ((voltage - 500mV) * 100) 31 return (voltage - 0.5) * 100; 32 }

The getTemperatureC function does the math necessary to convert from the data the sensor gives into the Celsius temperature. Since ouranalogIn() can return a value between 0 and 1023, we can calculate the voltage by multi- plying our reading by 5.0 and dividing it by 1024. The sensor that we are using sends 500mV at 0 Celsius (so that you can read negative temperatures.) It then goes up 10mV per degree C. For example, here is what the sensor will return for some different temperatures. Temperature Celsius Voltage from sensor -10 400mV 0 500mV 10 600mV 20 700mV 30 800mV 40 900mV 50 1000mV This is the first function we have written that returns a value. (Remember, all of the other functions have been of type void meaning they don't return a value.) You will see that to return the value you simply put return followed by the value to return. (Instead of a value, you can put a calculation like we have done here.) Returning a value means that when you call a function it has an "answer" that you can assign to a variable. We send that to the Serial Monitor and then we convert to Fahrenheit4 by calling convertToF(). This function takes the temperature in Celsius and converts it to Fahrenheit. ConvertingfromFahrenheittoCelsiusis formula: Fahrenheit = 9 5(Celsius)+ 32

34 float convertToF(float temperatureC)
35 { 36 return (temperatureC * 9.0 / 5.0) + 32.0; 37 }

4Only 2 countries in the world STILL use Fahrenheit as the main temperature scale. The US and Belize.

5.3 Hooking up the LCD

LCD stands for Liquid Crystal Display. We will refer to it as either an LCD or simply a display.

There are a large number of different LCDs available. They come in all shapes and sizes. Some can display characters (letters and numbers) only and others can display graphics (pictures).

For this book, we are using an 84x48 graphical LCD. (That means that there are 84 pixels (dots) across and 48 pixels down.) Controlling an LCD directly would be very difficult, so most LCDs have a controller chip attached. This one has a PCD8544 for its controller.

In this chapter, we will just hook it up and use some routines to put text on the display. In the next chapter, we will explore what we can do a little more and put some graphics on the display as well.

You may have noticed that we have the LCD connected to a small PCB (printed circuit board) with another chip on it. That is because the LCD works at 3.3V and we are running the Arduino at 5V. The chip on the PCB does the voltage conversion for us so we won't damage the LCD.

There are 8 pins on the board. Here is a list of the pins and what they do:

Pin Description GND This connects to Ground on the Arduino 3.3V Connect to the 3.3V power on the Arduino. This is power for the LCD. VERY important that this is connected to 3.3V and NOT 5V or you could damage the LCD. CLK The serial clock5 DIN This is where the serial6 data is sent D/C This lets the LCD know whether what is being sent to it is a command or data CS This is the Chip Select.7 For this book, we will always tie it to GND RST This resets the controller on the LCD. LED Controls the backlight. We can connect it to +5V to be always on, or GND to be always off, or to a pin to be able to turn it on or off. 8 Now let's hook up the circuit.

1. Place the LCD + PCB into the breadboard where the pins that are labeled on the purple PCB are in a4-a11.

The purpose of the serial clock is it lets the controller know when to look at DN for the next bit 6serial means it is sent one bit at a time When this is low then the chip is listening to D/C, DIN, CLK, and RST) This can either be tied to Ground (which will make it always listen) or used so that the pins can also be used for other purposes. Yes, we can even use PWM like we have earlier to have different brightness levels of the backlight.

2. Connect the far right column to GND on the Arduino.

3. Connect the next to right column to +5V on the Arduino.

4. Connect c4 to the far right column (ground).

5. Connect c5 to the 3V3 on the Arduino. (VERY IMPORTANT! DOUBLE CHECK before adding power.)

6. Connect c6 (CLK) to pin 5 on the Arduino.

7. Connect c7 (DIN) to pin 6 on the Arduino.

8. Connect c8 (D/C) to pin 7 on the Arduino.

9. Connect c9 (CS) to the far right column (ground). 9

10. Connect c10 (RST) to pin 8 on the Arduino.

11. Connect c11 (LED) to the next to right column (+5V). This means that the backlight will always be on.

5.4 Talking to the LCD

While we could write all of the code to talk to the LCD, we are going to use some functions in a library. A library is a collection of code that can be used by multiple programs. This allows us to simply call functions that make it much easier to communicate with the LCD. If you are interested in how the LCD works, you can look inside the library but explaining that code is outside of the scope of this book.

This means that the LCD will always be listening on its pins.

5.4 Talking to the LCD

5.4.1 Installing the library

Create a directory called libraries within your sketchbook directory (Go to the Preferences menu item to see where your sketchbook directory is. Copy the files off the USB stick in the directory /libraries into the directory you just made.) If you don't have the USB stick, you can get the files from http://www.introtoarduino.com Then restart the Arduino IDE by quitting it and starting it over again. If you don't restart the Arduino IDE then you won't be able to use the library. The list of all of the functions in the library is in Appendix A.4.

5.4.2 Using the LCD

Like we have many times already, we will start with the whole program and then go through and discuss new parts.

Listing 5.3: lcd1/lcd1.pde

```
1 #include <PCD8544.h>

2 3 const int kPin_CLK = 5; 4 const int
kPin_DIN = 6; 5 const int kPin_DC = 7; 6
const int kPin_RESET = 8;
```

7 8 PCD8544 lcd(kPin_CLK, kPin_DIN, kPin_DC, kPin_RESET);

9 10 void setup() 11 { 12 lcd.init(); 13 lcd.setCursor(0,0); 14 lcd.print("Hello, World!"); 15 }

16 17 void loop() 18 { 19 lcd.setCursor(0,1); 20 lcd.print(millis());

21 }

So, the first thing you will notice that is new is in line 1.

1 #include <PCD8544.h>

The #include tells the computer to take the file mentioned and when it is "compiling" the program to replace the #includestatementwith the contents of that file. An #include can either have the angle brackets which means to look in the library directory or it can have quotes which means to look in the same directory that the sketch is in. The next few lines are our pin definitions. Then we create a variable of a new type.

8 PCD8544 lcd(kPin_CLK, kPin_DIN, kPin_DC, kPin_RESET);

In this statement we are defining a variable named lcd of type PCD854410 and telling the computer which pins are connected on the Arduino. To define the variable we tell it what pin clk, din, dc, and reset are attached to.

10 void setup() 11 { 12 lcd.init(); 13 lcd.setCursor(0,0); 14 lcd.print("Hello, World!"); 15 }

In line 12, we call lcd.init() which will initialize the lcd. After this has returned, we can use the lcd. In line 13, we set the cursor to the upper left of the screen. (There are 84 "columns" and 6 "lines" in this display. Just like in arrays, it starts at 0 instead of 1.) In line 14, we print a message. This is very similar to how we sent messages over serial earlier in this chapter except we use lcd.print instead of serial.print.

10PCD8544 is the name of the LCD controller we are using. How to create new types ofvariables is outside the scope of this book but is a feature supported by the language.

5.5 Bringing it all together

```
17 void loop() 18 { 19 lcd.setCursor(0,1);
20 lcd.print(millis()); 21 }
```

This is the code that is called over and over again. In line 19, we set the cursor to the 0th column (far left), and the 1st row. (Remember that it starts at 0 so this is really the 2nd row.) In line 20, we see a shortcut. We have usedmillis() before in section3.2.3. We could have done this with 2 lines of code like:

```
long      numMillis      =      millis();
lcd.print(numMillis);
```

However, in this case since we didn't need the value of the number of mil- liseconds for anything else, we just sent the result of the millis() function directly to lcd.print().

5.5 Bringing it all together

So now, lets combine the thermometer code we did earlier in the chapter with the lcd code we just used.

Listing 5.4: temp_lcd/temp_lcd.pde 1 #include <PCD8544.h>

```
2 3 const int kPin_CLK = 5; 4 const int
kPin_DIN = 6; 5 const int kPin_DC = 7; 6
```

```
const int kPin_RESET = 8; 7 const int kPin_Temp = A0;

8 9 PCD8544 lcd(kPin_CLK, kPin_DIN, kPin_DC, kPin_RESET);

10 11 void setup() 12 {

13 lcd.init(); 14 lcd.setCursor(10,0); 15 lcd.print("Temperature:"); 16 }

17 18 void loop() 19 { 20 float temperatureC = getTemperatureC(); 21 // now convert to Fahrenheit 22 float temperatureF = convertToF(temperatureC);

23 24 lcd.setCursor(21,1); 25 lcd.print(temperatureC); 26 lcd.print(" C"); 27 lcd.setCursor(21,2); 28 lcd.print(temperatureF); 29 lcd.print(" F"); 30 delay(100); 31 }

32 33 float getTemperatureC() 34 { 35 int reading = analogRead(kPin_Temp);

36 37 float voltage = (reading * 5.0) / 1024; 38 // convert from 10 mv per degree with 500mV offset 39 // to degrees ((voltage - 500mV) * 100) 40 return (voltage - 0.5) * 100; 41 }
```

42   43   float   convertToF(float temperatureC)   44   {   45   return (temperatureC * 9.0 / 5.0) + 32.0; 46 }

The only thing new and interesting in this program is that we used the set Cursor() function to put the text mostly centered on the screen.

Congratulations, you now have a digital thermometer that reports the temperature in Celsius and Fahrenheit!

1. Change the program so it displays the voltage returned from the sensor as well as the temperature in Celsius and Fahrenheit.

2. Change the program so it displays the temperature in Fahrenheit as well as the maximum and minimum temperatures it has seen.

3. CHALLENGE: Modify the program in exercise 2 to also show how long ago (in seconds) the minimum and maximum temperature were seen.

Conclusion

Thank you again for downloading this book!

I hope this book was able to help you to you started on the road to creating things using micro-controllers.

Finally, if you enjoyed this book, then I'd like to ask you for a favor, would you be kind enough to leave a review for this book on Amazon? It'd be greatly appreciated!

Thank you and good luck!

I truly do appreciate it!

Best Wishes,

Byron Francis

59534159R00054

Made in the USA
Lexington, KY
08 January 2017